BOOKS BY OGDEN NASH

HARD LINES (1931)
FREE WHEELING (1931)
HAPPY DAYS (1933)
FOUR PROMINENT SO AND SO'S (1934)
THE PRIMROSE PATH (1935)
THE BAD PARENTS' GARDEN OF VERSE (1936)
I'M A STRANGER HERE MYSELF (1938)
GOOD INTENTIONS (1942)
VERSUS (1949)

THE PRIVATE DINING ROOM (1953)
YOU CAN'T GET THERE FROM HERE (1957)
EVERYONE BUT THEE AND ME (1962)
SANTA GO HOME: A CASE HISTORY FOR PARENTS (1967)
THERE'S ALWAYS ANOTHER WINDMILL (1968)
THE OLD DOG BARKS BACKWARDS (1972)

COLLECTED AND SELECTED

THE FACE IS FAMILIAR (1940)
MANY LONG YEARS AGO (1945)
FAMILY REUNION (1950)
VERSES FROM 1929 ON (1959)
MARRIAGE LINES: NOTES OF A STUDENT HUSBAND (1964)
BED RIDDANCE: A POSY FOR THE INDISPOSED (1970)

AVE OGDEN: NASH IN LATIN (TRANSLATED BY JAMES C. GLEESON AND BRIAN N. MEYER) (1973)
I WOULDN'T HAVE MISSED IT: SELECTED POEMS OF OGDEN NASH (1975)
A PENNY SAVED IS IMPOSSIBLE (1981)

FOR CHILDREN

THE CRICKET OF CARADOR (WITH JOSEPH ALGER) (1925)
MUSICAL ZOO (WITH TUNES BY VERNON DUKE) (1947)
PARENTS KEEP OUT: ELDERLY POEMS FOR YOUNGERLY READERS (1951)
THE CHRISTMAS THAT ALMOST WASN'T (1957)
CUSTARD THE DRAGON (1959)
A BOY IS A BOY: THE FUN OF BEING A BOY (1960)
CUSTARD THE DRAGON AND THE WICKED KNIGHT (1961)

THE NEW NUTCRACKER SUITE AND OTHER INNOCENT VERSES (1962)
GIRLS ARE SILLY (1962)
A BOY AND HIS ROOM (1963)
THE ADVENTURES OF ISABEL (1963)
THE UNTOLD ADVENTURES OF SANTA CLAUS (1964)
THE ANIMAL GARDEN (1965)
THE CRUISE OF THE AARDVARK (1967)
THE MYSTERIOUS OUPHE (1967)
THE SCROOBIOUS PIP (BY EDWARD LEAR; COMPLETED BY OGDEN NASH) (1968)
CUSTARD AND COMPANY (1980)

FOR THE THEATER

ONE TOUCH OF VENUS (WITH S. J. PERELMAN) (1944)

EDITED BY OGDEN NASH

NOTHING BUT WODEHOUSE (1932)
THE MOON IS SHINING BRIGHT AS DAY: AN ANTHOLOGY OF GOOD-HUMORED VERSE (1953)

I COULDN'T HELP LAUGHING: STORIES SELECTED AND INTRODUCED (1957)
EVERYBODY OUGHT TO KNOW: VERSES SELECTED AND INTRODUCED (1961)

A PENNY SAVED IS IMPOSSIBLE

A PENNY SAVED IS IMPOSSIBLE

BY OGDEN NASH

WITH DRAWINGS BY KEN MARYANSKI

LITTLE, BROWN AND COMPANY
BOSTON TORONTO LONDON

Library of Congress Cataloging in Publication Data

Nash, Ogden, 1902–1971.
    A penny saved is impossible.

    I. Title.
PS3527.A637P4 1981   811'.52   81–13742
ISBN 0–316–59832–1   AACR2

10 9 8 7 6 5 4

BP

Designed by Janis Capone

*Published simultaneously in Canada
by Little, Brown & Company (Canada) Limited*

PRINTED IN THE UNITED STATES OF AMERICA

CONTENTS

=

Part One: EVERY DAY IS MONDAY

Part Two: LINES INDITED WITH ALL THE DEPRAVITY OF POVERTY

Part Three: A MAN CAN COMPLAIN, CAN'T HE?

PART ONE
EVERY DAY IS MONDAY

GRASSHOPPERS ARE VERY INTELLIGENT

Ah woe, woe, woe, man was created to live by the sweat of his
    brow,
And it doesn't make any difference if your brow was moist
    yesterday and the day before, you've still got to get it
    moist again right now,
And you know deep in your heart that you will have to
    continue keeping it dewy
Right up to the time that somebody at the club says, I suppose
    we ought to go to what's-his-name's funeral, who won
    the fifth at Bowie?
That's a nasty outlook to face,
But it's what you get for belonging to the human race.
So far as I know, mankind is the only section of creation
That is doomed to either pers- or ex-piration.
Look at the birds flying around, and listen to them as their
    voices in song they hoist;
No wonder they sing so much, they haven't got any brows,
    and if they had they couldn't be bothered keeping them
    moist.
And bees don't do anything either, bees just have a reputation
    for industry because they are sharp enough to buzz,
And people hear a bee buzzing and don't realize that buzzing
    isn't any trouble for a bee so they think it is doing more
    than it actually does,
So next time you are about to expend some enthusiasm on the
    bee's wonderful industrial powers,
Just remember that that wonderful bee would die laughing if
    you asked it to change places with you and get its brow
    moist while you went around spending the day smell-
    ing flowers.

Oh yes, and the flowers, they seem to get along all right
    without being overactive,
All they do is sit around looking attractive,
And furthermore, if you can believe all you hear,
They only get up energy enough to do that about once a year
Thus we see that if you are botany
Your life is just an everlasting spell of pleasant monotony,
But if you are humanity, it is far from so,
And that is why I exclaim Woe woe woe,
Because I don't see much good in being the highest form of life
If all you get out of it is a brow moist from perpetual struggle
    and strife.
Indeed sometimes when my brow is particularly moist I think
    I would rather be a humble amœba
Than Solomon in all his glory entertaining the Queen of
    Sheba.

EVERY DAY IS MONDAY

Monday is the day that everything starts all over again,
Monday is the day when just as you are beginning to feel
      peaceful you have to get up and get dressed and put on
      your old gray bonnet and drive down to Dover again,
It is the day when life becomes grotesque again,
Because it is the day when you have to face your desk again.
When the telephone rings on Saturday or Sunday you are
      pleased because it probably means something pleasing
      and you take the call with agility,
But when it rings on any other day it just usually means some
      additional responsibility,
And if in doubt,
Why the best thing to do is to answer it in a foreign accent or if
      you are a foreigner answer it in a native accent and say
      you are out.
Oh, there is not a weekday moment that can't wring a sigh
      from you,
Because you are always being confronted with people who
      want to sell you something, or if they don't want to sell
      you something, there is something they want to buy
      from you,
And every shining hour swaggers arrogantly up to you
      demanding to be improved,
And apparently not only to improve it, but also to shine it, is
      what you are behooved.
Oh for a remedy, oh for a panacea, oh for a something, oh yes,
      oh for a coma or swoon,
Yes indeed, oh for a coma that would last from nine A.M. on
      Monday until Saturday noon.

SONG BEFORE BREAKFAST

Hopeful each morning I arise
And splash the cobwebs from my eyes.
I brush my teeth and scrape my chin
And bravely at the mirror grin.
Sternly I force myself to say,
Huzza! huzza! another day!
Oh happy me! oh lucky I!
Another chance with life to vie!
Another golden opportunity
To rise and shine in this community!
Another target for my aim!
Another whack at wealth and fame!
Almost I feel within me stir
A budding force of character.
Who knows, indeed, but what I might
Perhaps have altered overnight?
Today may be the day, who knows,
That sees me triumph o'er my foes:
Gluttony, simony, and sloth,
And drawing on the table cloth;
Perjury, arson, envy, pride,
And renting tales of homicide;
Barratry, avarice, and wrath,
And blowing bubbles in the bath.
The differences this day may bring!
Perhaps I'll work like anything;
I'll travel to my tasks on foot,
And in the bank the carfare put,
And buy a haircut when I need it,
And if I get a letter, read it,
And every eve improve myself
By inching through the Five Foot Shelf.

The things I want to do, I won't,
And only do the things I don't.
What lordly aspirations dawn
The while I draw my trousers on!
On beamish morning, big with hope
And noble tasks with which to cope,
If I should fail you, do not sorrow;
I'll be a better man tomorrow.

WILL CONSIDER SITUATION

These here are words of radical advice for a young man
    looking for a job;
Young man, be a snob.
Yes, if you are in search of arguments against starting at the
    bottom,
Why I've gottom.
Let the personnel managers differ;
It's obvious that you will get on faster at the top than at the
    bottom because there are more people at the bottom
    than at the top so naturally the competition at the
    bottom is stiffer.
If you need any further proof that my theory works,
Well, nobody can deny that presidents get paid more than
    vice-presidents and vice-presidents get paid more than
    clerks.
Stop looking at me quizzically;
I want to add that you will never achieve fortune in a job that
    makes you uncomfortable physically.
When anybody tells you that hard jobs are better for you than
    soft jobs be sure to repeat this text to them,
Postmen tramp around all day through rain and snow just to
    deliver people's in cozy air-conditioned offices checks
    to them.
You don't need to interpret tea leaves stuck in a cup
To understand that people who work sitting down get paid
    more than people who work standing up.
Another thing about having a comfortable job is you not only
    accumulate more treasure;
You get more leisure.
So that when you find you have worked so comfortably that
    you waistline is a menace,
You correct it with golf or tennis.

8

Whereas if in an uncomfortable job like piano-moving or
    stevedoring you indulge,
You have no time to exercise, you just continue to bulge.
To sum it up, young man, there is every reason to refuse a job
    that will make heavy demands on you corporally or
    manually,
And the only intelligent way to start your career is to accept a
    sitting position paying at least twenty-five thousand
    dollars annually.

PROCRASTINATION IS
ALL OF THE TIME

===

Torpor and sloth, torpor and sloth,
These are the cooks that unseason the broth.
Slothor and torp, slothor and torp
The directest of bee-line ambitions can warp.
He who is slothic, he who is torporal,
Will not be promoted to sergeant or corporal.
No torporer drowsy, no comatose slother
Will make a good banker, not even an author.
Torpor I deprecate, sloth I deplore,
Torpor is tedious, sloth is a bore.
Sloth is a bore, and torpor is tedious,
Fifty parts comatose, fifty tragedious.
How drear, on a planet redundant with woes,
That sloth is not slumber, nor torpor repose.
That the innocent joy of not getting things done
Simmers sulkily down to plain not having fun.
You smile in the morn like a bride in her bridalness
At the thought of a day of nothing but idleness.
By midday you're slipping, by evening a lunatic,
A perusing-the-newspapers-all-afternoonatic,
Worn to a wraith from the half-hourly jaunt
After glasses of water you didn't want,
And at last when onto your pallet you creep,
You discover yourself too tired to sleep.
O torpor and sloth, torpor and sloth,   ·
These are the cooks that unseason the broth.
Torpor is harrowing, sloth it is irksome —
Everyone ready? Let's go out and worksome.

WHERE THERE'S A WILL,
THERE'S VELLEITY

≡

Seated one day at the dictionary I was pretty weary and also
pretty ill at ease,

Because a word I had always liked turned out not to be a word
at all, and suddenly I found myself among the *v*'s,

And suddenly among the *v*'s I came across a new word which
was a word called *velleity*,

So the new word I found was better than the old word I lost,
for which I thank my tutelary deity,

Because *velleity* is a word which gives me great satisfaction,

Because do you know what it means, it means *low degree of
volition not prompting to action*,

And I always knew I had something holding me back but I
didn't know what,

And it's quite a relief to know it isn't a conspiracy, it's only
velleity that I've got,

Because to be wonderful at everything has always been my
ambition,

Yes indeed, I am simply teeming with volition,

So why I never was wonderful at anything was something I
couldn't see

While all the time, of course, my volition was merely volition
of a low degree,

Which is the kind of volition that you are better off without
it,

Because it puts an idea in your head but doesn't prompt you to
do anything about it.

So you think it would be nice to be a great pianist but why
bother with practicing for hours at the keyboard,

Or you would like to be the romantic captain of a romantic
ship but can't find time to study navigation or charts of
the ocean or the seaboard;

You want a lot of money but you are not prepared to work for
    it,
Or a book to read in bed but you do not care to go into the
    nocturnal cold and murk for it;
And now if you have any such symptoms you can identify
    your malady with accurate spontaneity:
It's velleity,
So don't forget to remember that you're velleitous, and if
    anybody says you're just lazy,
Why, they're crazy.

A STITCH TOO LATE IS MY FATE

≡

There are some people of whom I would certainly like to be
      one,
Who are the people who get things done.
They balance their checkbooks every month and their figures
      always agree with the bank's,
And they are prompt in writing letters of condolence or
      thanks.
They never leave anything to chance,
But always make reservations in advance.
When they get out of bed they never neglect to don slippers so
      they never pick up athlete's foot or a cold or a splinter,
And they hang their clothes up on hangers every night and put
      their winter clothes away every summer and their
      summer clothes away every winter.
Before spending any money they insist on getting an estimate
      or a sample,
And if they lose anything from a shoelace to a diamond ring it
      is covered by insurance more than ample.
They have budgets and what is more they live inside of them,
Even though it means eating things made by recipes clipped
      from the Sunday paper that you'd think they would
      have died of them.
They serve on committees
And improve their cities.
They are modern knight errants
Who remember their godchildren's birthdays and the anniver-
      saries of their godchildren's parents,
And in cold weather they remember the birds and supply
      them with sunflower seed and suet,
And whatever they decide to do, whether it's to save twenty-
      five percent of their salary or learn Italian or write a
      musical comedy or touch their toes a hundred times

every morning before breakfast, why they go ahead
and do it.
People who get things done lead contented lives, or at least I
guess so,
And I certainly wish that either I were more like them or they
were less so.

CAT NAPS ARE TOO GOOD FOR CATS

≡

Oh, early every afternoon
I like a temporary swoon.
I do not overeat at luncheon,
I do not broach the bowl or puncheon;
Yet the hour from two to three
Is always sleepy-time to me.

Bolt upright at my desk I sit,
My elbows digging into it,
My chin into my hands doth fit,
My careful fingers screen my eyes,
And all my work before me lies,
Which leads inquisitive passer-bys
Who glance my way and see me nod,
To think me wide awake, if odd.

I would not sell my daily swoon
For all the rubies in Rangoon.
What! sell my swoon? My lovely swoon?
Oh, many and many's the afternoon
I've scoured the woods with Daniel Boone,
And sipped a julep with Lorna Doone
And Former Governor Ruby Laffoon.
I'll sell my soul before my swoon,
It's not for sale, my swoon's immune.

From two to three each afternoon
Mine are the Mountains of the moon,
Mine a congenital silver spoon.
And I can lead a lost platoon
Or dive for pearls in a haunted lagoon,
Or guide a stratosphere balloon.

Oh, where the schooner schoons, I schoon,
I can talk lion, or baboon,
Or make a crooner cease to croon.
I like to swoon, for when I swoon
The universe is my macaroon.
Then blessings on thee, my afternoon torpor,
Thou makest a prince of a mental porpor.

OH TO BE ODD!

≡

Hypochondriacs
Spend the winter at the bottom of Florida and the summer on
      top of the Adirondriacs.
You go to Paris and live on champagne wine and cognac
If you're a dipsomognac.
If you're a manic-depressive
You don't go anywhere where you won't be cheered up, and
      people say "There, there!" if your bills are excessive.
But you stick around and work day and night and night and
      day with your nose to the sawmill
If you're nawmill.

TWO SONGS FOR A BOSS NAMED
MR. LONGWELL

≡

I

Put it there, Mr. Longwell, put it there!
You're a bear, Mr. Longwell, you're a bear!
It's our verdict
That your service is perfect.
You're a regular American crusader
And you'll lick old H. L. Mencken's Armada.
You know life isn't all a picnic
But it hasn't made you a cynic.
From first to last
As the banner goes past
We'll sing our favorite air.
Our choice always narrows
To the man you can't embarrass,
So put it there, Mr. Longwell, put it there!

II

L for loyalty to his grand old firm,
O for his eyes of blue,
N for his ideals and his spirit of cooperation,
G for his influence on me and you.
W for his ability to collect and coordinate facts,
E–L–L for the laborsaving card-index system he put through.
Put them all together, they spell LONGWELL,
Which is about what you might expect them to do.

19

SPRING COMES TO MURRAY HILL

≡

I sit in an office at 244 Madison Avenue,
And say to myself You have a responsible job, havenue?
Why then do you fritter away your time on this doggerel?
If you have a sore throat you can cure it by using a good
      goggeral,
If you have a sore foot you can get it fixed by a chiropodist,
And you can get your original sin removed by St. John the
      Bopodist,
Why then should this flocculent lassitude be incurable?
Kansas City, Kansas, proves that even Kansas City needn't
      always be Missourible.
Up up my soul! This inaction is abominable.
Perhaps it is the result of disturbances abdominable.
The pilgrims settled Massachusetts in 1620 when they landed
      on a stone hummock.
Maybe if they were here now they would settle my stomach.
Oh, if I only had the wings of a bird
Instead of being confined on Madison Avenue I could soar in a
      jiffy to Second or Third.

LET GEORGE DO IT,
IF YOU CAN FIND HIM

The wind comes walloping out of the West,
And the sky is lapis lazuli,
And the hills are bold in red and gold,
And I cannot take it casually.
Oh, cruel day for a man to spend
At counter or desk or forge!
I think I shall stray from duty today,
And turn it over to George.

George! George! Where are you, George?
Clear the air for a call to George!
There is work to be done, dear George,
And fame to be won, dear George!
There are words to write,
And columns to add,
And everyone says
That George is the lad.
Here is a pen and here is a pencil,
Here's a typewriter, here's a stencil,
Here is a list of today's appointments,
And all the flies in all the ointments,
The daily woes that a man endures —
Take them, George, they're yours!

I will arise and roam the fields
Where edible coveys flutter,
I will conquer, methinks, the perilous links
With a true and deadly putter.
I'll forsake the grime of the city street
For valley and hill and gorge;
I will, or would, or I shall, or should,
But I can't get hold of George!

George! George! Were are you, George?
Come out from under the sofa, George!
I thought you were braver, George!
I'm doing you a favor, George!
You can use my desk,
And sit in my chair,
Snugly away
From the nasty air.
Safe from the other fellow's cartridges,
Safe from returning without any partridges,
Safe from treacherous spoons and brassies,
And the flaming shorts of the golfing lassies.
All this, dear George, I am trying to spare you.
George! You softie, where are you?

MR. ARTESIAN'S
CONSCIENTIOUSNESS

≡

Once there was a man named Mr. Artesian and his activity
     was tremendous,
And he grudged every minute away from his desk because the
     importance of his work was so stupendous;
And he had one object all sublime,
Which was to save simply oodles of time.
He figured that sleeping eight hours a night meant that if he
     lived to be seventy-five he would have spent twenty-
     five years not at his desk but in bed,
So he cut his slumber to six hours which meant he only lost
     eighteen years and nine months instead,
And he figured that taking ten minutes for breakfast and
     twenty minutes for luncheon and half an hour for
     dinner meant that he spent three years, one month and
     fifteen days at the table,
So that by subsisting solely on bouillon cubes which he
     swallowed at his desk to save this entire period he was
     able,
And he figured that at ten minutes a day he spent a little over
     six months and ten days shaving,
So he grew a beard, which gave him a considerable saving,
And you might think that now he might have been satisfied,
     but no, he wore a thoughtful frown,
Because he figured that at two minutes a day he would spend
     thirty-eight days and a few minutes in elevators just
     traveling up and down,
So as a final timesaving device he stepped out the window of
     his office, which happened to be on the fiftieth floor,
And one of his partners asked "Has he vertigo?" and the other
     glanced out and down and said "Oh no, only about ten
     feet more."

———

MORE ABOUT PEOPLE

===

When people aren't asking questions
They're making suggestions
And when they're not doing one of those
They're either looking over your shoulder or stepping on your
 toes
And then as if that weren't enough to annoy you
They employ you.
Anybody at leisure
Incurs everybody's displeasure.
It seems to be very irking
To people at work to see other people not working,
So they tell you that work is wonderful medicine,
Just look at Firestone and Ford and Edison,
And they lecture you till they're out of breath or something
And then if you don't succumb they starve you to death or
 something.
All of which results in a nasty quirk:
That if you don't want to work you have to work to earn
 enough money so that you won't have to work.

PORTRAIT OF THE ARTIST AS A
PREMATURELY OLD MAN

≡

It is common knowledge to every schoolboy and even every
    Bachelor of Arts,
That all sin is divided into two parts.
One kind of sin is called a sin of commission, and that is very
    important,
And it is what you are doing when vou are doing something
    you ortant,
And the other kind of sin is just the opposite and is called a sin
    of omission and is equally bad in the eyes of all
    right-thinking people, from Billy Sunday to Buddha,
And it consists of not having done something you shuddha.
I might as well give you my opinion of these two kinds of sin
    as long as, in a way, against each other we are pitting
    them,
And that is, don't bother your head about sins of commission
    because however sinful, they must at least be fun or
    else you wouldn't be committing them.
It is the sin of omission, the second kind of sin,
That lays eggs under your skin.
The way you get really painfully bitten
Is by the insurance you haven't taken out and the checks you
    haven't added up the stubs of and the appointments
    you haven't kept and the bills you haven't paid and the
    letters you haven't written.
Also, about sins of omission there is one particularly painful
    lack of beauty,
Namely, it isn't as though it had been a riotous red-letter day
    or night every time you neglected to do your duty;
You didn't get a wicked forbidden thrill
Every time you let a policy lapse or forgot to pay a bill;

You didn't slap the lads in the tavern on the back and loudly
      cry Whee,
Let's all fail to write just one more letter before we go home,
      and this round of unwritten letters is on me.
No, you never get any fun
Out of the things you haven't done,
But they are the things that I do not like to be amid,
Because the suitable things you didn't do give you a lot more
      trouble than the unsuitable things you did.
The moral is that it is probably better not to sin at all, but if
      some kind of sin you must be pursuing,
Well, remember to do it by doing rather than by not doing.

DANCE UNMACABRE

This is the witching hour of noon;
Bedlam breaks upon us soon.
When the stroke of twelve has tolled
What a pageant doth unfold.
Drawers slam on pads of notes,
Eager fingers clutch at coats;
Compact, lipstick, comb and hat,
Here a dab and there a pat;
The vital letter just begun
Can sulk in the machine till one.
Stenographers on clicking heels
Scurry forth in quest of meals;
Secretaries arm in arm
Fill the corridors with charm;
The stolid air with scent grows heavy
As bevy scuttles after bevy;
Like the pipers on the beach,
Calling shrilly each to each,
Sure as arrows, swift as skaters,
Converging at the elevators.
From the crowded lift they scatter
Bursting still with turbulent chatter;
The revolving door in rapture whirls
Its quarters full of pretty girls.
Soignée, comme il faut and *chic*
On forty or forty-five a week.
When One upon the dial looms
They hurry to their office tombs,
There to bide in dust till five,
When they come again alive.

WE'LL ALL FEEL BETTER BY WEDNESDAY

≡

I love coffee, I love tea,
I love the girls, but they're mean to me.
I love Saturday, I love Sunday,
But how could anyone ever love Monday?
Let's make a scientific analysis,
Let's diagnose this Monday paralysis.
Well, you've suffered an overdose of sunburn;
You must blister and peel before you un-burn.
For junk your muscles could all be sold for,
From engaging in games you are now too old for.
You're bloated from a diet of buns and hamburgers,
Chickenburgers, cheeseburgers, nutburgers, clam-
    burgers.
Your hair may be brushed, but your mind's untidy,
You've had about seven hours' sleep since Friday,
No wonder you feel that lost sensation;
You're sunk from a riot of relaxation.
What you do on weekends, you claim to adore it.
But Monday's the day that you suffer for it.
That's why Labor Day is a red-letter news day —
Blue Monday doesn't come until Tuesday.

≡

I hardly suppose I know anybody who wouldn't rather be a
 success than a failure,
Just as I suppose every piece of crabgrass in the garden would
 much rather be an azalea,
And in celestial circles all the run-of-the-mill angels would
 rather be archangels or at least cherubim and seraphim,
And in the legal world all the little process-servers hope to
 grow up into great big bailiffim and sheriffim.
Indeed, everybody wants to be a wow,
But not everybody knows exactly how.
Some people think they will eventually wear diamonds instead
 of rhinestones
Only by everlastingly keeping their noses to their ghrine-
 stones,
And other people think they will be able to put in more time at
 Palm Beach and the Ritz
By not paying too much attention to attendance at the office
 but rather in being brilliant by starts and fits.
Some people after a full day's work sit up all night getting a
 college education by correspondence,
While others seem to think they'll get just as far by devoting
 their evenings to the study of the difference in tempera-
 ment between brunettance and blondance.
In short, the world is filled with people trying to achieve
 success,
And half of them think they'll get it by saying No and half of
 them by saying Yes,
And if all the ones who say No said Yes, and vice versa, such is
 the fate of humanity that ninety-nine percent of them
 still wouldn't be any better off than they were before,
Which perhaps is just as well because if everybody was a
 success nobody could be contemptuous of anybody

else and everybody would start in all over again trying to be a bigger success than everybody else so they would have somebody to be contemptuous of and so on forevermore,

Because when people start hitching their wagons to a star,

That's the way they are.

I YIELD TO MY LEARNED BROTHER
OR
IS THERE A CANDLESTICK MAKER IN THE HOUSE?

===

The doctor gets you when you're born,
The preacher, when you marry,
And the lawyer lurks with costly clerks
If too much on you carry.
Professional men, they have no cares;
Whatever happens, they get theirs.

You can't say When
To professional men,
For it's always When to they;
They go out and golf
With the big bad wolf
In the most familiar way.
Hard times for them contain no terrors;
Their income springs from human errors.

The noblest lord is ushered in
By a practicing physician,
And the humblest lout is ushered out
By a certified mortician.
And in between, they find their foyers
Alive with summonses from lawyers.

Oh, would my parents long ago
Had memorized this motto!
For then might I, their offspring, buy
A Rolls or an Isotto.
But now I fear I never can,
For I am no professional man.

You can't say When
To professional men,
For it's always When to they;
They were doing fine
In '29,
And they're doing fine today.

INTROSPECTIVE REFLECTION

≡

I would live all my life in nonchalance and insouciance
Were it not for making a living, which is rather a nouciance.

PART TWO
LINES INDITED WITH ALL THE DEPRAVITY OF POVERTY

FIRST PAYMENT DEFERRED

Let us look into the matter of debt
Which is something that the longer you live, why the deeper
into it you get,
Because in the first place every creditor is his debtor's keeper,
And won't let you get into debt in the first place unless you are
capable of getting in deeper,
Which is an unfortunate coincidence
Because every debtor who is capable of getting deeper into
debt is attracted only to creditors who will encourage
him to get deeper into debt, which is a most fabulous
and unfair You-were-a-creditor-in-Babylon-and-I-was-
a-Christian-debtor Elinor Glyncidence.
Some debtors start out with debts which are little ones,
Such as board and lodging and victual ones;
Other debtors start out by never demanding that their bills be
itemized,
Which means that they are bitten by little creditors upon the
backs of bigger creditors and are so on ad infinitum-
ized.
Veteran debtors dabble in stocks,
Or their families get adenoids or appendicitis or pox,
Any of which means that debt is what they get beneather and
beneather,
Either to them who told them about the stocks or to them who
administer the chloroform and ether.
Some debts are fun while you are acquiring them,
But none are fun when you set about retiring them,
So you think you will reform, you think instead of sinking into
debt you will ascend into credit,
So you live on a budget and save twenty-five percent of your
salary and cut corners and generally audit and edit,

And that is the soundest idea yet,
Because pretty soon your credit is so good that you can charge
anything you want and settle down for eternity into
peaceful and utterly irremediable debt.

ONE FROM ONE LEAVES TWO

≡

Higgledy piggledy, my black hen,
She lays eggs for gentlemen.
Gentlemen come every day
To count what my black hen doth lay.
If perchance she lays too many,
They fine my hen a pretty penny;
If perchance she fails to lay,
The gentlemen a bonus pay.

Mumbledy pumbledy, my red cow,
She's cooperating now.
At first she didn't understand
That milk production must be planned;
She didn't understand at first
She either had to plan or burst,
But now the government reports
She's giving pints instead of quarts.

Fiddle de dee, my next-door neighbors,
They are giggling at their labors.
First they plant the tiny seed,
Then they water, then they weed,
They they hoe and prune and lop,
Then they raise a record crop,
Then they laugh their sides asunder,
And plow the whole caboodle under.

Abracadabra, thus we learn
The more you create, the less you earn.
The less you earn, the more you're given,
The less you lead, the more you're driven,
The more destroyed, the more they feed,

The more you pay, the more they need,
The more you earn, the less you keep,
And now I lay me down to sleep.

I pray the Lord my soul to take
If the tax collector hasn't got it before I wake.

BANKERS ARE JUST LIKE ANYBODY ELSE, EXCEPT RICHER

≡

This is a song to celebrate banks,
Because they are full of money and you go into them and all
    you hear is clinks and clanks,
Or maybe a sound like the wind in the trees on the hills,
Which is the rustling of the thousand-dollar bills.
Most bankers dwell in marble halls,
Which they get to dwell in because they encourage deposits
    and discourage withdralls,
And particularly because they all observe one rule which woe
    betides the banker who fails to heed it,
Which is you must never lend any money to anybody unless
    they don't need it.
I know you, you cautious conservative banks!
If people are worried about their rent it is your duty to deny
    them the loan of one nickel, yes, even one copper
    engraving of the martyred son of the late Nancy
    Hanks;
Yes, if they request fifty dollars to pay for a baby you must
    look at them like Tarzan looking at an uppity ape in the
    jungle,
And tell them what do they think a bank is, anyhow, they had
    better go get the money from their wife's aunt or ungle.
But suppose people come in and they have a million and they
    want another million to pile on top of it,
Why, you brim with the milk of human kindness and you urge
    them to accept every drop of it,
And you lend them the million so then they have two million
    and this gives them the idea that they would be better
    off with four,
So they already have two million as security so you have no
    hesitation in lending them two more,

And all the vice-presidents nod their heads in rhythm,
And the only question asked is do the borrowers want the
      money sent or do they want to take it withm.
But please do not think that I am not fond of banks,
Because I think they deserve our appreciation and thanks,
Because they perform a valuable public service in eliminating
      the jackasses who go around saying that health and
      happiness are everything and money isn't essential,
Because as soon as they have to borrow some unimportant
      money to maintain their health and happiness they
      starve to death so they can't go around anymore
      sneering at good old money, which is nothing short of
      providential.

MS. FOUND UNDER A SERVIETTE
IN A LOVELY HOME

≡

. . . Our outlook is totally different from
that of our American cousins, who have never
had an aristocracy. Americans relate all
effort, all work, and all of life itself to the dollar.
Their talk is of nothing but dollars.
The English seldom sit happily chatting for
hours on end about pounds.
— NANCY MITFORD IN Noblesse Oblige

Dear Cousin Nancy:

You probably never heard of me or Cousin Beauregard or
Cousin Yancey,

But since you're claiming kin all the way across the ocean, we
figure you must be at least partwise Southern,

So we consider you not only our kith and kin but also our
kithin' couthern.

I want to tell you, when Cousin Emmy Lou showed us your
piece it stopped the conversation flat,

Because I had twenty dollars I wanted to talk about, and
Cousin Beauregard had ten dollars he wanted to talk
about, and Cousin Yancey didn't have any dollars at all,
and he wanted to talk about that.

But Cousin Emmy Lou looked over her spectacles, which the
common people call glasses,

And she offered us a dollar to stop talking about dollars and
start talking about the English upper classes.

Cousin Beauregard wanted to know why the English aristocra-
cy was called English when most of their names were
French to begin with,

And now anybody with an English name like Hobbs or Stobbs
has to accumulate several million of those pounds they
seldom chat about, to buy his way in with.

Cousin Yancey said he could understand that — the St. Au-
byns beat the hell out of the Hobbses in 1066 — but

there was a more important point that he could not determine,

Which is why the really aristocratic English aristocrats have names that are translated from the German.

Cousin Emmy Lou is pretty aristocratic herself; in spite of her weakness for hog jowl and potlikker, she is noted for her highborn pale and wan flesh,

And where most people get gooseflesh she gets swan flesh,

And she said she thought you ought to know that she had been over the royal roster

And she had spotted at least one impostor.

She noticed that the Wicked Queen said "Mirror, mirror on the wall" instead of "Looking glass, looking glass on the wall," which is perfectly true,

So the Wicked Queen exposed herself as not only wicked but definitely non-U.

After that, we all loosened our collars

And resumed our conversation about dollars.

IF HE WERE ALIVE TODAY, MAYHAP,
MR. MORGAN WOULD SIT ON THE
MIDGET'S LAP

Beep-beep.

BANKERS TRUST AUTOMOBILE LOAN
You'll find a banker at Bankers Trust
— ADVERTISEMENT IN
N.Y. Times

When comes my second childhood.
As to all men it must,
I want to be a banker
Like the banker at Bankers Trust.
I wouldn't ask to be president,
Or even assistant veep,
I'd only ask for a kiddie car
And permission to go beep-beep.

The banker at Chase Manhattan,
He bids a polite Good-day;
The banker at Immigrant Savings
Cries *Scusi!* and *Olé!*
But I'd be a sleek Ferrari
Or perhaps a joggly jeep,
And scooting around at Bankers Trust,
Beep-beep, I'd go, beep-beep.

The trolley car used to say clang-clang
And the choo-choo said toot-toot,
But the beep of the banker at Bankers Trust
Is every bit as cute.
Miaow, says the cuddly kitten,
Baa, says the woolly sheep,
Oink, says the piggy-wiggy,
And the banker says beep-beep.

So I want to play at Bankers Trust
Like a hippety-hoppy bunny,
And best of all, oh best of all,
With really truly money.
Now grown-ups dear, it's nightie-night
Until my dream comes true,
And I bid you a happy boop-a-doop
And a big beep-beep *adieu*.

LINES INDITED WITH ALL THE DEPRAVITY OF POVERTY

===

One way to be very happy is to be very rich
For then you can buy orchids by the quire and bacon by the
    flitch.
And yet at the same time
People don't mind if you only tip them a dime.
Because it's very funny
But somehow if you're rich enough you can get away with
    spending water like money
While if you're not rich you can spend in one evening your
    salary for the year
And everybody will just stand around and jeer.
If you are rich you don't have to think twice about buying a
    judge or a horse,
Or a lower instead of an upper, or a new suit, or a divorce.
And you never have to say When,
And you can sleep every morning until nine or ten,
All of which
Explains why I should like very, very much to be very, very
    rich.

FRAGONARD

≡

There was an old miser named Clarence,
Who simonized both of his parents.
"The initial expense,"
He remarked, "is immense,
But I'll save it on wearance and tearance."

I CAN'T STOP UNLESS YOU STOP
OR
LINES ADDRESSED TO A MAN MAKING $5,000 A YEAR WHO OVERTIPS A MAN MAKING $10,000 A YEAR TO MAKE HIMSELF FEEL HE'S MAKING $20,000 A YEAP

═══

I do not wish to tiptoe through the tulips to Tipperary,
And I might vote for Tyler too, but about Tippecanoe I am a
     little wary.
The fact is, that at any mention of any form of tips,
My mind goes into an eclipse.
The world of tips has moved too fast for me,
The price of ransoming my hat has become too vast for me.
I have to get used to one thing at a time,
And just as I learn that there is no more such tip as a nickel, I
     find that there is no more such tip as a dime.
If you give a dime to a bellhop,
The skyscrapers buck like broncos, and you can almost feel the
     hotel hop.
If you want to talk to bellhops or porters,
You start with baby-talk, which is quarters.
If you want to talk to headwaiters, or, as they now style
     themselves, maître d's,
You talk in C's or G's,
And the girl with the tray of cigarettes expects the Taj Mahal,
And not a small Mahal, either, but a large Mahal.
This is a sad situation for low and middle income persons,
And when you go abroad, it worsens.
At least on the trains over here
You don't have to tip the conductor and the engineer,
And over here, certainly until recently, it would have been
     considered impudent effrontery

───

52

To tip the President of the country,
Whereas, in certain nations that shall be nameless,
The entire citizenry is shameless.
Granted that itching palms
Know no qualms,
Nevertheless people, whether men or mice,
Resent scratching the same palm twice,
Which happens wherever you eat or sleep, on the continent,
    because a fat percentage is added to the bill to cover all
    tips,
But if you think that no further tipping is expected, you'd
    better learn to carry your own pemmican and balance
    your baggage on your hips.
Oh dear, I think that extravagant tips are an unnecessary
    menace,
Whether in Valdosta, Georgia, or Valparaiso, or Vancouver,
    or Venice.
I think that they are a betrayal of the tipper's unsure ego, or
    not quite-quiteness,
I think that they are a vulgar substitute for common polite-
    ness.
I think that people could do very well both at home and abroad
    on moderate gratuities or fees
If they would just take the trouble to learn and employ the
    foreign and domestic terms for Thank you, and Please.

THE TERRIBLE PEOPLE

≡

People who have what they want are very fond of telling
    people who haven't what they want that they really
    don't want it,
And I wish I could afford to gather all such people into a
    gloomy castle on the Danube and hire half a dozen
    capable Draculas to haunt it.
I don't mind their having a lot of money, and I don't care how
    they employ it,
But I do think that they damn well ought to admit they enjoy
    it.
But no, they insist on being stealthy
About the pleasures of being wealthy,
And the possession of a handsome annuity
Makes them think that to say how hard it is to make both ends
    meet is their bounden duity.
You cannot conceive of an occasion
Which will find them without some suitable evasion.
Yes indeed, with arguments they are very fecund;
Their first point is that money isn't everything, and that they
    have no money anyhow is their second.
Some people's money is merited,
And other people's is inherited,
But wherever it comes from,
They talk about it as if it were something you got pink gums
    from.
Perhaps indeed the possession of wealth is constantly dis-
    tressing,
But I should be quite willing to assume every curse of wealth if
    I could at the same time assume every blessing.
The only incurable troubles of the rich are the troubles that
    money can't cure,

Which is a kind of trouble that is even more troublesome if you
     are poor.
Certainly there are lots of things in life that money won't buy,
     but it's very funny —
Have you ever tried to buy them without money?

THE SECOND MONTH IT'S NOT
ITEMIZED

I go to my desk to write a letter,
A simple letter without any frills;
I can't find space to write my letter,
My desk is treetop high in bills.

I go to my desk to write a poem
About a child of whom I'm afraid;
I can't get near it to write my poem
For the barrel of bills, and all unpaid.

I go to my desk for an aspirin tablet,
For a handy bottle of syrup of squills,
I reach in the drawer for the trusty bicarbonate;
My fingers fasten on nothing but bills.

I go to my desk to get my checkbook
That checks may blossom like daffodils,
Hundreds of checks to maintain my credit;
I can't get through the bills to pay my bills.

I've got more bills than there are people,
I've got bigger bills than Lincoln in bronze,
I've got older bills than a Bangor & Aroostook day
        coach,
I've got bills more quintuplicate than Dionnes.

There's a man named Slemp in Lima, Ohio,
Since 1930 he has been constantly ill,
And of all the inhabitants of this glorious nation
He is the only one who has never sent me a bill.

The trouble with bills, it costs money to pay them,
But as long as you don't, your bank is full.
I shall now save some money by opening a charge
    account
With a fuller, a draper, and a carder of wool.

NATURE ABHORS A VACANCY

An ordeal of which I easily tire
Is that of having a lease expire.
Where to unearth another residence?
You can't have the White House, that's the President's.
You scour the Bowery, ransack the Bronx,
Through funeral parlors and honky-tonks.
From river to river you comb the town
For a place to lay your family down.
You find one, you start to hoist your pennant,
And you stub your toe on the previous tenant.
He's in bed with croup, his children have gout,
And you can't push in until they pull out,
And when they pull out, the painters take on
And your date with the movers has come and gone,
So your furniture in storage sits
While you camp out royally at the Ritz.
When leases expire, one wish I've got,
To be a landlord, and live on a yacht.

WE WOULD REFER YOU
TO OUR SERVICE DEPARTMENT,
IF WE HAD ONE

=

It fills me with elation
To live in such a mechanical-minded nation,
Surrounded not only by the finest scenery
But also the most machinery,
Where every prospect is attractive
And people are radioactive,
Reading books with show-how
Written by scientists with know-how.
Breathes there with soul so dead a fossil
Who never to himself hath said, Production is colossal?
Obviously civilization is far from a crisis
When the land teems with skilled craftsmen skillfully manu-
    facturing gadgets and mechanical devices.
Millions of washing machines and electric refrigerators
Are shipped from the shipping rooms of their originators,
Streamlined dreamlined automobiles roll off the assembly
    lines in battalions and droves,
Millions of radios pour from the factories for housewives to
    listen to in the time they save through not having to
    slice their pre-sliced loaves,
So when everybody has a houseful and a garageful of mechani-
    cal perfection no one has any worries, but if you want a
    worry, I will share one,
Which is, Why is it that when seemingly anybody can make
    an automobile or a washing machine, nobody can
    repair one?
If you want a refrigerator or an automatic can opener or a razor
    that plays "Begin the Beguine" you can choose between
    an old rose or lavender or blue one,

But after you've got it, why if anything goes wrong don't think
you'll find anybody to fix it, just throw it away and buy
a new one.
Oh well, anyhow here I am nearly forty-five,
And still alive

THAR SHE BLOWS

≡

Indoors or out, no one relaxes
In March, that month of wind and taxes,
The wind will presently disappear,
The taxes last us all the year.

PRIDE GOETH BEFORE A RAISE
OR
AH, THERE, MRS.
CADWALLADER-SMITH!

The Cadwallader-Smiths
Are People with Poise;
I consider them one of the minor joys,
Though frequently wishing
That I could share
Their imperturbable *savoir-faire*.

Madame is a modishly youthful matron,
Artfully dyed and I think enameled;
Monsieur is a generous opera patron,
A Man-about-Town, by trade untrammeled.
Oh the dapper dandies,
The haughty dames,
In the phalanx of hy-
Phenated names!
(Have you ever observed
That the name of Smith
Is the oftenest hy-
Phenated with?)
Now come the junior Cadwallader-Smiths,
Those perennial rotogravurian myths,
Maidens who scale the Alps and Rockies,
Debutantes with the world in tow,
Polo players and gentleman jockeys,
And athletes tailored in Savile Row.
Oh glamorous girls and golden boys,
They practically palpitate with poise!
Say me a word. It's a word they've got.
So what?

Well, though hardly copy for a great biographer,
They know how to twinkle for a news photographer.
They don't go to work, but they wallow in shekels,
And they sit on beaches and don't get freckles.
They exchange divorces without bearing malice,
And they all get presented at Buckingham Palace.
They receive reporters with a nonchalant air,
And they're dignified even in the barber chair,
They are dignified even in their testimonials
To beautifying lotions for the crude Colonials.
They take a paper and they read the headlines,
So they've heard of unemployment and they've heard of
        breadlines,
And they philanthropically cure them all
By getting up a costume charity ball.
They tipple nectar and they nibble lotus,
And they pay no attention to a jury notus,
And they don't get a summons when they run past stoplights,
So they have the point of view of true cosmopolites.
They could all pay taxes, but they'd rather not.
So what?
Well, they're People with Poise,
The Cadwallader-Smiths,
With the sensitive senses of monoliths,
Which I freely admit
I could use myself,
Had I all I desire of profit and pelf.

A PENNY SAVED IS IMPOSSIBLE

≡

The further through life I drift
The more obvious it becomes that I am lacking in thrift.
Now thrift is such a boon to its possessor that years ago they
   began to tax it,
But it is a bane to him that lacks it
Because if you lack it you will go into a shoppe and pay two
   dollars for a gifte,
But if you possess it you find something just as good for a
   dollar fifte.
A penny is merely something that you pull several of out of
   your pocket before you find the nickel you need for a
   telephone call, if thriftlessness is in your blood,
Whereas to the thrifty a penny is something to be put out at
   stud.
Thrifty people put two-cent stamps on letters addressed to a
   three-cent zone,
And thriftless people on the other end pay the postage due and
   the thrifty people chuckle and rub their hands because
   the saving on every six letters represents a year's
   interest on a dollar loan.
Oh that I were thrifty, because thrifty people leave estates to
   delight their next of kin with;
Oh yes that I were thrifty, because then not only would I have
   money in the bank to pay my bills, but I could leave the
   money in the bank because I wouldn't have run up the
   bills to begin with;
Oh that I were not a spendthrift, oh then would my heart
   indeed be gladsome,
Because it is so futile being a spendthrift because I don't know
   any places where thrift could be spent even if I had
   some.

APARTMENT TO
SUBLET — UNFURNISHED

≡

The Murrays are hunting a house,
They are tired of living in flats.
They long for a personal mouse,
And a couple of personal cats.
They are hunting a house to inhabit,
An Eden, or even an Arden,
They are thinking of keeping a rabbit,
They are thinking of digging a garden.
How giddy the Murrays have grown,
To aspire to a house of their own!

Oh, hurry, hurry!
Says Mrs. Murray.
Tarry awhile, says he,
If you care for a house
As is a house,
You'd better leave it to me.
I'd like an orchard, apple or peach,
I'd like an accessible bathing beach,
And a den for unwinding detective plots,
And a lawn for practicing mashie shots,
And open fires,
And a pleasant sunroom,
A handy garage,
And perhaps a gunroom,
And an atmosphere exempt of static,
And a furnace silent and automatic.
For such a house
I would hurry, hurry —
I'm a practical man,
Says Mr. Murray.

The Murrays of 17 B,
The Murrays are going away,
From the wireless in 17 C,
And the parties in 17 A.
For the Murrays are tired of flats,
They are rapidly growing aloof,
As they dream of their personal cats,
As they dream of their personal roof.
Their friends cannot smother their merriment
When they speak of the Murrays' experiment.

Oh, hurry, hurry!
Says Mr. Murray.
Tarry awhile, says she.
When we choose a house,
Let us choose a house
As nice as a house can be.
With a dozen windows south and east,
And a dozen capacious cupboards at least,
And a laundry lilting with light and air,
And a porch for a lady to dry her hair,
And plenty of sun,
And plenty of shade,
And a neat little place
For a neat little maid,
And a wall with roses clambering wild,
And a quiet room for a sleepy child.
If you happen to see it,
Hurry, hurry!
For *that's* the house,
Says Mrs. Murray.

YOU HAVE MORE FREEDOM
IN A HOUSE

===

The Murrays have moved to a house,
They are finished forever with flats;
They longed for a personal mouse,
And room to swing dozens of cats.
They longed for a hearth and a doorway,
In Arden, or maybe in Eden,
But the Eden is rather like Norway,
And the Arden like winter in Sweden.
How baffled the Murrays have grown
Since they live in a house of their own!

Oh, hurry, hurry!
Says Mrs. Murray.
But listen, my dear, says he,
If you want the house
A temperate house,
You'd better not leave it to me.
I've learned the knack of swinging a cat,
But I can't coerce the thermostat.
The furnace has given a gruesome cough,
And something has cut the fuel off,
And the heart of the nursery radiator
Is cold as the nose of an alligator,
And I've telephoned for the service men
But they can't get here until after ten,
So swaddle the children,
And hurry, hurry —
I'm a practical man,
Says Mr. Murray.

The Murrays are vague about fuses,
And mechanical matters like that,
And each of them frequently muses
On the days when they lived in a flat.
Was the plumbing reluctant to plumb?
Was the climate suggestive of Canada?
Did the radio crackle and hum?
You simply called down to the janada!
The Murrays have found no replacement
For the genius who lived in the basement.

Oh, hurry, hurry!
Says Mr. Murray.
I'm doing my best, says she,
But it's hard to scrub
In a tepid tub,
So the guests must wait for me;
And tell them they'll get their cocktails later
When you've managed to fix the refrigerator.
And explain if the coffee looks like water,
That the stove is as queer as a seventh daughter,
And I will be down as soon as able
To unstick the drawers of my dressing table.

There's a car at the door, says Mrs. Murray,
The doorbell's broken, so hurry, hurry!
Oh, I don't regret
Being wed to you,
But I wish I could wed
A janitor too.

TO BARGAIN, TOBOGGAN, TO-WHOO!

There is one form of argument that though I am a voicer of I
    can't see the good of,
And that is, arguing that you can afford something you can't
    afford just because it doesn't cost much more than
    something you also can't afford would of.
You pass up going to the movies,
And then you suddenly pat yourselves on the back for passing
    them up and say we passed them up, therefore we can
    afford to take dinner out and order a lot of hors d'ovies,
And the dinner costs five dollars, but the movies would have
    cost seventy cents,
So the dinner only really cost four thirty which for the dinner
    you had is not so immense,
So then you say there is a new show opening tonight but we
    don't know whether it's good or terrible, so why take a
    chance,
So why not go out and dance?
So you go out and dance and the least you pay is ten dollars for
    cover charge plus elixir,
But on that basis you figure you are at least four dollars ahead
    on the evening because seats to an opening that any-
    body wants to see open are not to be had for a fiver or
    indeed a sixer,
So eventually you go to bed,
And you wake up in the morning with the glorious feeling that
    you are several dollars ahead,
So you start out the day being ahead by several dollars,
And then you read an advertisement saying that somebody has
    removed thirty percent from the price of their ties and
    socks and collars,
So although the ties and socks and collars you already have are
    still pretty clean,

Why you go in and order fifty dollars' worth because by
spending fifty dollars you can save fifteen,
So take the fifteen that you save on the ties and socks and
collars plus what you saved the night before and it is
obvious that you have saved about twenty,
Which for a twenty-four-hour thrift account strikes you as
plenty,
So then you really get the economical urge,
And then you really begin to splurge,
And you look on every splurge as a fairy godmother's gift
Because you charge it all up to thrift,
Because the more you spend, the more you save, so you
naturally spend enormous amounts,
Because whether you can pay for it or not, it's the principle of
thrift that counts,
So it ends up with your starting out by saving the seventy
cents that you would have squandered at your neigh-
borhood cinema,
And really and truly ends up by your saving two dollars or
two thousand, depending on whether you have spent
twenty dollars or twenty thousand to save it, which
just depends on your financial maxima and minima.

RING OUT THE OLD, RING IN THE NEW, BUT DON'T GET CAUGHT IN BETWEEN

≡

I. FIRST CHIME

If there is anything of which American industry has a
    superfluity
It is green lights, know-how, initiative and ingenuity.
If there is one maxim to American industry unknown
It is, Let well enough alone.
Some people award American industry an encomium
Because it not only paints the lily, it turns it into a two-toned
    job with a forward look and backward fins and a calyx
    trimmed with chromium.
I don't propose to engage in a series of Lincoln-Douglas
    debates,
But take the matter of paper plates.
The future of many a marriage would have been in doubt
But for paper plates, which have imparted tolerability to
    picnics and the maid's day out,
But the last paper plates I handled had been improved into
    plastic and they are so artistic that I couldn't throw
    them away,
And I ended up by washing them against another day.
Look at the automotive industry, how it never relaxes;
It has improved the low-priced three so much that instead of a
    thousand dollars they now cost twenty-nine seventy-
    five, not including federal and local taxes.
Do you know what I think?
Ordinary mousetraps will soon be so improved that they will
    be too good for the mice, who will be elbowed out by
    mink.

That low keening you hear is me bemoaning my fate;
I am out of joint, I was born either too early or too late.
As the boll said to the weevil,
Get yourself born before the beginning or after the end, but
    never in the middle of, a technological upheaval.
I am adrift, but know not whether I am drifting seaward or
    shoreward,
My neck is stiff from my head trying to turn simultaneously
    backward and forward.
One way I know I am adrift,
My left foot keeps reaching for the clutch when the car has an
    automatic shift.
Another way that I am adrift I know,
I'm in a car that I've forgotten has a clutch and I stall it when
    the light says Stop and again when the light says Go.
I find that when dressing I behave as one being stung by
    gallinippers
Because half my trousers are old style and half new and I am
    forever zipping buttons and buttoning zippers.
I can no longer enjoy butter on my bread;
Radio and TV have taught me to think of butter as "You know
    what" or "The more expensive spread."
I am on the thin ice of the old order while it melts;
I guess that perhaps in this changing world money changes less
    than anything else.
That is one reason money is to me so dear;
I know I can't take it with me, I just want the use of some
    while I am here.

≡

Solomon said, Stay me with apples for I am sick with *l'amour*,
But I say, Comfort me with flagons, for I am sick with rich
    people talking and acting poor.
I have never yet met even a minor Crœsus
Whose pocketbook didn't have paresis;
I have never yet been out with a tycoon for an evening in
    Manhattan's glamorous canyons
When the evening's bills weren't paid by the tycoon's impov-
    erished but proud companions.
There is one fact of life that no unwealthy child can learn too
    soon,
Which is that no tycoon ever spends money except on another
    tycoon.
Rich people are people that you owe something to and take out
    to dinner and the theater and dancing and all the other
    expensive things there are because you know they are
    accustomed to the best and as a result you spend the
    following month on your uppers,
And it is a big evening to you but just another evening to them
    and they return the hospitality by saying that someday
    you must drop in to one of their cold Sunday suppers.
Rich people are also people who spend most of their time
    complaining about the income tax as one of life's
    greatest and most intolerable crosses,
And eventually you find that they haven't even paid any
    income tax since 1929 because their income has shrunk
    to fifty thousand dollars a year and everything has been
    charged off to losses,
And your own income isn't income at all, it is salary, and stops
    coming in as soon as you stop laboring mentally and
    manually,

But you have been writing out checks for the government
 annually,
So the tax situation is just the same as the entertainment
 situation because the poor take their little pittance
And pay for the rich's admittance
Because it is a great truth that as soon as people have enough
 coupons in the safe-deposit vault or in the cookie jar on
 the shelf,
Why they don't have to pay anything themself,
No, they can and do just take all their coins and store them,
And other people beg to pay for everything for them,
And they certainly are allowed to,
Because to accept favors is the main thing that the poor are and
 the rich aren't too proud to,
So let us counterattack with sangfroid and phlegm,
And I propose a Twenty-second Amendment to the Constitu-
 tion providing that the rich must spend as much money
 on us poor as we do on them.

I'LL EAT MY SPLIT-LEVEL TURKEY
IN THE BREEZEWAY

≡

A lady I know disapproves of the vulgarization of Christmas;
    she believes that Christmas should be governed purely
    by spiritual and romantic laws;
She says all she wants for Christmas is no more suggestive
    songs about Santa Claus.
Myself, I am more greedy if less cuddle-y,
And being of '02 vintage I am perforce greedy fuddy-duddily,
So my own Christmas could be made glad
Less by the donation of anything new than just by the return
    of a few things I once had.
Some people strive for gracious living;
I have recurrent dreams of spacious living.
Not that I believe retrogression to be the be-all and the end-all,
Not that I wish to spend the holidays sitting in a Turkish
    corner smoking Sweet Caps and reading *Le Rouge et le
    Noir* by Stendhal,
Nor do I long for a castle with machicolations,
But I would like a house with a porte cochere so the guests
    wouldn't get wet if it rained the evening of my party for
    my rich relations.
Also, instead of an alcove I'd like a dining room that there
    wasn't any doubt of,
And a bathtub that you didn't have to send $7.98 to Wisconsin
    for a device that enables you to hoist yourself out of,
And if there is one thought at which every cockle of my heart
    perks up and warms,
It is that of an attic in which to pile old toys and magazines and
    fancy dress costumes and suitcases with the handle off
    and dressmaker's forms.
I'd like a house full of closets full of shelves,

And above all, a house with lots of rooms all with doors that shut so that every member of the family could get off alone by themselves.

Please find me such a relic, dear Santa Claus, and when you've done it,

Please find me an old-fashioned cook and four old-fashioned maids at $8.00 a week and a genial wizard of a handyman to run it.

ROULETTE US BE GAY

≡

The trouble with games of chance is that they don't do much
    to stimulate your pulse
Unless you risk some money on the results,
And the trouble with playing for money is not that it is a sin,
But that you have got either to lose or win,
And the trouble with losing is not only that you need the
    money, which is an important point, very true,
But also that you never lose it except to somebody who is very
    much richer than you,
And the trouble with winning, if you can bring yourself to
    imagine any trouble with winning, is that except in the
    most glamorous fiction
You never win except from somebody to whom you know that
    the money that they pay over to you is all that stands
    between them and eviction.
Another thing about games of chance
Is a thing at which I look askance,
And that is that no matter how far at any time you may be
    ahead,
You are always well behind when it is time for bed,
While on the other hand if you start out by losing as steadily
    and heavily as if you were afflicted with Tutankhamen's
    curse
You finish up even worse,
So you can take it as understood
That your luck changes only if it's good.
And this, my friends, is a brief history of the major troubles
    with gambling but I feel that no improving lesson from
    it will be learned
As long as there is nothing so delightful in the world as money
    you haven't earned.

MONEY IS EVERYTHING

===

Better a parvenu
Living luxuriously on Park Arvenu
Than a Schuyler or a Van Rensselaer
Living inexpensselaer.

I BURN MONEY

The song about the happy-go-lucky fellow who hasn't time to
    be a millionaire strikes me as pretty funny,
Because I am pretty happy-go-lucky myself but it isn't lack of
    time that keeps me from being a millionaire, it's lack of
    money,
But if anybody has a million that they're through with it,
Well, I know what I'd like to do with it.
My first acquisition would not be a lot of Old Masters or first
    editions or palatial palaces,
No, it would be to supply each of my pairs of pants with its
    own set of galluses.
I can also think of another extravagance with which to startle
    all beholders
Which is an attendant with no other duties than to apply
    antisunburn lotion to that vulnerable spot you can't get
    at yourself either by reaching over or under your
    shoulders.
Likewise I have an idea which should earn the gratitude of
    every regular-dinner eater alive,
Which is to promote a regular-dinner that when you order
    oysters or clams on it you get six oysters or clams
    instead of five.
My next goal is one to reach which I should probably have to
    sink into debt,
But it would be worth it because it is the development of a
    short, hot, harsh, quick-burning, full-of-nicotine ciga-
    rette.
A million dollars could also be well spent in hiring somebody
    to invent some better rhymes for wife than rife and
    knife and strife,

But I think what I would really do if I had a million would be to buy a million dollars' worth of books written by me and then besides having a lot of good books I could sit back and live on the royalties for the rest of my life.

THE SONG OF SONGS

≡

Is anybody here in favor of a redistribution of wealth?

Because I think it ought to be redistributed, only not by force
or by stealth,

Because it is only when other people have it and you haven't
that it is evil,

So we had better try to correct the situation before it is made
worse by a revolution or an upheaval.

Let us not be like the Soviets and fall prey to any communistic
demagog,

No, surely we have more sense than a mujik and would yawn
at arguments that keep them agog;

And let us not be sheep like a Fascist audience

Who get played on by their leaders like concertinas or
accaudience;

Let us rather correct in our own 100% American way the
wrongs that annoy and disgust us,

And correct them so the corrections will not offend the
Constitution and Mr. Hughes, our imposing Chief
Justice;

Let us handle it in the manner of Washington and Jefferson and
Jackson

And keep very levelheaded and Anglo-Saxon.

There are several things standing in the way of a natural
distribution of wealth, but if you want to know which
is the chief thing, well, I will tell you which:

The rich marry only the rich.

It is one of our national disasters

That, broadly speaking, Astors and Vanderbilts and Rockefel-
lers and Morgans never marry anybody but Morgans
and Rockefellers and Vanderbilts and Astors,

Whereas if they only bestowed their affections on somebody
in a lower crust,

Why money would be distributed over this broad land of ours
like dust,
So I think they may all be rich but honest,
But I think their matchmaking proclivities ought to be har-
nessed.
Yes, if money marrying money were prohibited,
How speedily and how painlessly it would be redistributed.
Yes, yes, the rich and the poor can settle and forget their
differences just as the Blue and the Gray have
As soon as we have a law saying that people can only marry
people who have a lot less money than they have,
And that will be the end of all your present and future
Townsends and Coughlins and Longs,
And that is why I call this piece the Song of Songs.

PART THREE
A MAN CAN COMPLAIN, CAN'T HE?

REFLECTION ON THE FALLIBILITY
OF NEMESIS

≡

He who is ridden by a conscience
Worries about a lot of nonscience;
He without benefit of scruples
His fun and income soon quadruples.

A BAS BEN ADHEM

My fellow man I do not care for.
I often ask me, What's he there for?
The only answer I can find
Is, Reproduction of his kind.
If I'm supposed to swallow that,
Winnetka is my habitat.
Isn't it time to carve Hic Jacet
Above that Reproduction racket?

To make the matter more succinct:
Suppose my fellow man extinct.
Why, who would not approve the plan
Save possibly my fellow man?
Yet with a politician's voice
He names himself as Nature' cnoice.

The finest of the human race
Are bad in figure, worse in face.
Yet just because they have two legs
And come from storks instead of eggs
They count the spacious firmament
As something to be charged and sent.

Though man created smocks and snoods
And one-way streets and breakfast foods,
And double features and mustard plasters,
And Huey Longs and Lady Astors,
He hails himself with drum and fife
And bullies lower forms of life.

Not that I think that much depends
On how we treat our feathered friends,

Or claim the wart hog in the zoo
Is nearer God than me or you;
Just that I wonder, as I scan,
The wherefore of my fellow man.

GOOD-BY, OLD YEAR, YOU OAF
OR
WHY DON'T THEY PAY THE BONUS?

≡

Many of the three hundred and sixty-five days of the year are
    followed by dreadful nights but one night is by far, oh
    yes, by far the worst,

And that, my friends, is the night of December the thirty-
    first.

Man can never get it through his head that he is born to be not
    a creditor but a debtor;

Man always thinks the annual thought that just because last
    year was terrible next year is bound to be better.

Man is a victim of dope

In the incurable form of hope;

Man is a blemishless Pollyanna,

And is convinced that the advent of every New Year will place
    him in possession of a bumper crop of manna.

Therefore Man fills himself up with a lot of *joie de vivre*

And goes out to celebrate New Year's *Ivre*.

Therefore millions of respectable citizens who just a week
    before have been perfectly happy to sit at home and be
    cozily Christmas carolized

Consider it a point of honor to go out on the town and get
    themselves paralyzed;

Therefore the whistles blow toot toot and the bells ring ding
    ding and the confetti goes confetti confetti at midnight
    on the thirty-first of December,

And on January first the world is full of people who either
    can't and wish they could, or can and wish they
    couldn't remember.

They never seem to learn from experience;

They keep on doing it year after year from the time they are
    puling infants till they are doddering octogenerience.

My goodness, if there's anything in heredity and environment

How can people expect the newborn year to manifest any culture or refironment?

Every New Year is the direct descendant, isn't it, of a long line of proven criminals?

And you can't turn it into a philanthropist by welcoming it with cocktails and champagne any more successfully than with prayer books and hyminals.

Every new year is a country as barren as the old one, and it's no use trying to forage it;

Every new year is incorrigible; then all I can say is for Heaven's sakes, why go out of your way to incorrage it?

ARE YOU A SNODGRASS?

≡

It is possible that most individual and international social and
economic collisions
Result from humanity's being divided into two main divisions.
Their lives are spent in mutual interference,
And yet you cannot tell them apart by their outward appear-
ance.
Indeed the only way in which to tell one group from the other
you are able
Is to observe them at the table,
Because the only visible way in which one group from the
other varies
Is in its treatment of the cream and sugar on cereal and berries.
Group A, which we will call the Swozzlers because it is a very
suitable name, I deem,
First applies the sugar and then swozzles it all over the place
pouring on the cream,
And as fast as they put the sugar on they swozzle it away,
But such thriftlessness means nothing to ruthless egotists like
they,
They just continue to scoop and swozzle and swozzle and
scoop,
Until there is nothing left for the Snodgrasses, or second
group.
A Snodgrass is a kind, handsome intelligent person who pours
the cream on first,
And then deftly sprinkles the sugar over the cereal or berries
after they have been properly immersed,
Thus assuring himself that the sugar will remain on the cereal
and berries where it can do some good, which is his
wish,
Instead of being swozzled away to the bottom of the dish.

———

The facts of the case for the Snodgrasses are so self-evident
that it is ridiculous to debate them,

But this is unfortunate for the Snodgrasses as it only causes the
sinister and vengeful Swozzlers all the more to hate
them.

Swozzlers are irked by the superior Snodgrass intelligence and
nobility

And they lose no opportunity of inflicting on them every kind
of incivility.

If you read that somebody has been run over by an automobile

You may be sure that the victim was a Snodgrass, and a
Swozzler was at the wheel.

Swozzlers start wars and Snodgrasses get killed in them,

Swozzlers sell waterfront lots and Snodgrasses get malaria
when they try to build in them.

Swozzlers invent fashionable diets and drive Snodgrasses
crazy with tables of vitamins and calories,

Swozzlers go to Congress and think up new taxes and Snod-
grasses pay their salaries,

Swozzlers bring tigers back alive and Snodgrasses get eaten by
anacondas,

Snodgrasses are depositors and Swozzlers are absconders,

Swozzlers hold straight flushes when Snodgrasses hold four of
a kind,

Swozzlers step heavily on the toes of Snodgrasses' shoes as
soon as they are shined.

Whatever achievements Snodgrasses achieve, Swozzlers al-
ways top them;

Snodgrasses say Stop me if you've heard this one, and
Swozzlers stop them.

Swozzlers are teeming with useful tricks of the trade that are
not included in standard university curricula;

The world in general is their oyster, and Snodgrasses in
particular.

So I hope for your sake, dear reader, that you are a Swozzler,
but I hope for everybody else's sake that you are not,

And I also wish that everybody else was a nice amiable Snodgrass too, because then life would be just one long sweet harmonious mazurka or gavotte.

POSSESSIONS ARE NINE POINTS
OF CONVERSATION

Some people, and it doesn't matter whether they are paupers
    or millionaires,
Think that anything they have is the best in the world just
    because it is theirs.
If they happen to own a 1921 jalopy,
They look at their neighbor's new deluxe convertible like the
    wearer of a 57th Street gown at a 14th Street copy.
If their seventeen-year-old child is still in the third grade they
    sneer at the graduation of the seventeen-year-old chil-
    dren of their friends,
Claiming that prodigies always come to bad ends,
And if their roof leaks,
It's because the shingles are antiques.
Other people, and it doesn't matter if they are Scandinavians
    or Celts,
Think that anything is better than theirs just because it
    belongs to somebody else.
If you congratulate them when their blue-blooded Doberman
    pinscher wins the obedience championship, they look
    at you like a martyr,
And say that the garbage man's little Rover is really infinitely
    smarter;
And if they smoke fifteen-cent cigars they are sure somebody
    else gets better cigars for a dime.
And if they take a trip to Paris they are sure their friends who
    went to Old Orchard had a better time.
Yes, they look on their neighbor's ox and ass with covetousness
    and their own ox and ass with abhorrence,
And if they are wives they want their husband to be like
    Florence's Freddie, and if they are husbands they want
    their wives to be like Freddie's Florence.

I think that comparisons are truly odious, I do not approve of this constant proud or envious to-do;

And furthermore, dear friends, I think that you and yours are delightful and I also think that me and mine are delightful too.

NATURE KNOWS BEST

===

I don't know exactly how long ago Hector was a pup,
But it was quite long ago, and even then people used to have to start their day by getting up.
Yes, people have been getting up for centuries,
They have been getting up in palaces and Pullmans and penitentiaries.
The caveman had to get up before he could go out and track the brontosaurus,
Verdi had to get up before he could sit down and compose the Anvil Chorus,
Alexander had to get up before he could go around being dominant,
Even Rip Van Winkle had to get up from one sleep before he could climb the mountain and encounter the sleep which has made him prominent.
Well, birds are descended from birds, and flowers are descended from flowers,
And human beings are descended from generation after generation of ancestors who got up at least once every twenty-four hours,
And because birds are descended from birds they don't have to be forced to sing like birds, instead of squeaking like rats,
And because flowers are descended from flowers they don't have to be forced to smell like flowers, instead of like burning rubber or the Jersey flats,
But you take human beings, why their countless generations of ancestors who were always arising might just as well have spent all their lives on their mattresses or pallets,
Because their descendants haven't inherited any talent for getting up at all, no, every morning they have to be forced to get up either by their own conscience or somebody else's, or alarm clocks or valets.

___

Well, there is one obvious conclusion that I have always held
to,
Which is that if Nature had really intended human beings to
get up, why they would get up naturally and wouldn't
have to be compelled to.

A MAN CAN COMPLAIN, CAN'T HE?
(A LAMENT FOR THOSE
WHO THINK OLD)

Pallid and moonlike in the smog,
Now feeble Phoebus 'gins arise;
The upper floors of Empire State
Have vanished into sooty skies.
Half missing, like the shrouded tower,
Lackluster, like the paten solar,
I draw reluctant waking breath;
Another day, another dolor.

That breath I draw was first exhaled
By diesel and incinerator;
I should have wakened not at all,
Or, were it feasible, even later.
Walls of the world close in on me,
Threats equatorial and polar;
Twixt pit and pendulum I lie;
Another day, another dolor.

Here's news about the current strike,
The latest, greatest test of fission,
A fatal mugging in the park,
An obit of the Geneva mission.
One envelope yields a baffling form
Submitted by the tax comptroller;
A jury summons completes my mail;
Another day, another dolor.

Once eager for, I've come to dread
The nimble fingers of my barber;
He's training strands across my scalp

Like skimpy vines across an arbor.
The conversation at the club
Is all intestinal or molar;
What dogs the Class of '24?
Another day, another dolor.

Between the dotard and the brat
My disaffection veers and varies;
Sometimes I'm sick of clamoring youth,
Sometimes of my contemporaries.
I'm old too soon, yet young too long;
Could Swift himself have planned it droller?
Timor vitae conturbat me;
Another day, another dolor.

YOUR LEAD, PARTNER, I HOPE
WE'VE READ THE SAME BOOK

≡

When I was just a youngster,
Hardly bigger than a midge,
I used to join my family
In a game of auction bridge
We were patient with reneging,
For the light was gas or oil,
And our arguments were settled
By a reference to Hoyle.
Auction bridge was clover;
Then the experts took it over.
You could no longer bid by the seat of your pants,
The experts substituted skill for chance.

The experts captured auction
With their lessons and their books,
And the casual weekend player
Got a lot of nasty looks.
The experts captured auction
And dissected it, and then
Somebody thought up contract,
And we played for fun again.
It was pleasant, lose or win,
But the experts muscled in,
And you couldn't deal cards in your own abode
Without having memorized the latest code.

We turned to simpler pastimes
With our neighbors and our kin;
Oklahoma or canasta,
Or a modest hand of gin.
We were quietly diverted

Before and after meals,
Till the experts scented suckers
And came yapping at our heels.
Behold a conquered province;
I'm a worm, and they are robins.
On the grandchildren's table what books are displayed?
Better Slapjack, and *How to Win at Old Maid*.

In a frantic final effort
To frivol expert-free,
I've invented Amaturo
For just my friends and me.
The deck has seven morkels
Of eleven guzzards each,
The game runs counterclockwise,
With an extra kleg for dreech,
And if you're caught with a gruice,
The score reverts to deuce.
I'll bet that before my cuff links are on the bureau
Some expert will have written *A Guide to Amaturo*.

THE ANATOMY OF HAPPINESS

===

Lots of truisms don't have to be repeated but there is one that
has got to be,

Which is that it is much nicer to be happy than it is not to be,

And I shall even add to it by stating unequivocally and
without restraint

That you are much happier when you are happy than when
you ain't.

Some people are just naturally Pollyanna,

While others call for sugar and cream and strawberries on their
manna.

Now, I think we all ought to say a fig for the happiness that
comes of thinking helpful thoughts and searching your
soul,

The most exciting happiness is the happiness generated by
forces beyond your control,

Because if you just depend on your helpful thoughts for your
happiness and would just as soon drink buttermilk as
champagne, and if mink is no better than lapin to you,

Why you don't even deserve to have anything nice and
exciting happen to you.

If you are really Master of your Fate,

It shouldn't make any difference to you whether Cleopatra or
the Bearded Lady is your mate,

So I hold no brief for the kind of happiness or the kind of
unhappiness that some people constantly carry around
in their breast,

Because that kind of happiness simply consists of being
resigned to the worst just as that kind of unhappiness
consists of being resentful of the best.

No, there is only one kind of happiness that I take the stump
for,

Which is the kind that comes when something so wonderful
     falls in your lap that joy is what you jump for,
Something not of your own doing,
When the blue sky opens and out pops a refund from the
     Government or an invitation to a terrapin dinner or an
     unhoped for yes from the lovely creature you have been
     disconsolately wooing.
And obviously such miracles don't happen every day,
But here's hoping they may,
Because then everybody would be happy except the people
     who pride themselves on creating their own happiness
     who as soon as they saw everybody who didn't create
     their own happiness happy they would probably grieve
     over sharing their own heretofore private sublimity,
A condition which I could face with equanimity.

INVOCATION

=

Smoot Plans Tariff Ban on Improper Books
— NEWS ITEM

Senator Smoot (Republican, Ut.)
Is planning a ban on smut.
Oh root-ti-toot for Smoot of Ut.
And his reverent occiput.
Smite, Smoot, smite for Ut.,
Grit your molars and do your dut.,
Gird up your l—ns,
Smite h—p and th—gh,
We'll all be Utah
By and by.

Smite, Smoot, for the Watch and Ward,
For Hiram Johnson and Henry Ford,
For Bishop Cannon and John D., Junior,
For Governor Pinchot of Pennsylvunia,
For John S. Sumner and Elder Hays
And possibly Edward L. Bernays,
For Orville Poland and Ella Boole,
For Mother Machree and the Shelton pool.
When smut's to be smitten
Smoot will smite
For G—d, for country,
And Fahrenheit.

Senator Smoot is an institute
Not to be bribed with pelf;
He guards our homes from erotic tomes
By reading them all himself.
Smite, Smoot, smite for Ut.,

They're smuggling smut from Balt. to Butte!
Strongest and sternest
Of your s–x
Scatter the scoundrels
From Can. to Mex.!

Smite, Smoot, for Smedley Butler,
For any good man by the name of Cutler,
Smite for the W.C.T.U.,
For Rockne's team and for Leader's crew,
For Florence Coolidge and Admiral Byrd,
For Billy Sunday and John D., Third,
For Grantland Rice and for Albie Booth,
For the Woman's Auxiliary of Duluth,
Smite, Smoot,
Be rugged and rough,
Smut if smitten
Is front-page stuff.

EVERYBODY TELLS ME EVERYTHING

≡

I find it very difficult to enthuse
Over the current news.
Just when you think that at least the outlook is so black that it
      can grow no blacker, it worsens,
And that is why I do not like to get the news, because there has
      never been an era when so many things were going so
      right for so many of the wrong persons.

MOST DOCTORS RECOMMEND
OR
YOURS FOR FAST FAST FAST RELIEF

===

They say that when cigarette advertising was banned from the
air the networks lost a cool billion in billing,
And at first they felt like their tooth had just lost a filling,
But they soon reflected that the cavity would be more than
refilled with a rich amalgam of et cetera such as
laxatives and deodorants,
And they viewed the situation with more forbearance and less
forboderance.
They said it might have been worse, and drank to the future in
Smirnoff or Beefeater or Gilbey.
They said it might have been worse; I say that with any luck it
will be.
When it comes to supposing, I am a man without a scruple,
So let us suppose that in the first year off the air the
consumption of cigarettes should double or quadruple.
Would not the producers of other goods begin to think twice?
And wouldn't that be nice?
Good wine needs no bush,
And perhaps products that people really want need no
hard-sell or soft-sell TV push.
Why not?
Look at pot.

A CLEAN CONSCIENCE
NEVER RELAXES

There is an emotion to which we are most of us adduced,
But it is one which I refuse to boost.
It is harrowing, browbeating, and brutal,
Besides which it is futile.
I am referring, of course,
To remorse.
Remorse is a violent dyspepsia of the mind,
But it is very difficult to treat because it cannot even be
    defined,
Because everything is not gold that glisters and everything is
    not a tear that glistens,
And one man's remorse is another man's reminiscence,
So the truth is that as far as improving the world is concerned,
    remorse is a duffer,
Because the wrong people suffer,
Because the very fact that they suffer from remorse proves
    they are innocuous,
Yes indeed, it is the man remorse passes over completely who
    is the virulent streptococcuous.
Do you think that when Nero threw a martyr to the lions
    remorse enveloped him like an affinity?
Why, the only remorse in the whole Colosseum was felt by
    the martyr who was reproaching himself for having
    dozed through the sermon on the second Sunday after
    Trinity.
So I think remorse ought to stop biting the consciences that
    feed it,
And I think the Communist Party ought to work out some
    plan for taking it away from those who have it and
    giving it to those who need it.

I SPY

=

Now elbow-deep in middle age,
A viewer I'm of video,
And some of it is beautiful,
But most of it is hideo.

I like to view the video
On Saturdays, for instance.
I like to cheer the Notre Dames,
The Rutgerses and Princetons.

I like to view Citation run,
I like to view his jockey,
I like to view the baseball game,
I like to view the hockey.

But there are less exalted scenes
I view upon the video,
The lady wrestlers make me sick.
Perhaps I'm too fastideo.

And evening vaudevideo,
I view it with alarum,
I can't determine which it's for,
The nursery or the barum.

Yet ask me to your house to view,
And I'll be there immidiate,
For all the world is video,
And I the village videot.

THE POLITICIAN

Behold the politician
Self-preservation is his ambition.
He thrives in the D. of C.,
Where he was sent by you and me.

Whether elected or appointed
He considers himself the Lord's anointed,
And indeed the ointment lingers on him
So thick you can't get your fingers on him.

He has developed a sixth sense
About living at the public expense,
Because in private competition
He would encounter malnutrition.

He has many profitable hobbies
Not the least of which is lobbies.
He would not sell his grandmother for a quarter
If he suspected the presence of a reporter.

He gains votes ever and anew
By taking money from everybody and giving it to a few,
While explaining that every penny
Was extracted from the few to be given to the many.

Some politicians are Republican, some Democratic,
And their feud is dramatic,
But except for the name
They are identically the same

LOOK FOR THE SILVER LINING

≡

I can't say that I feel particularly one way or the other towards
    bellboys,
But I do admit that I haven't much use for the it's-just-as-well
    boys,
The cheery souls who drop around after every catastrophe and
    think they are taking the curse off
By telling you about somebody who is even worse off.
No matter how deep and dark your pit, how dank your
    shroud,
Their heads are heroically unbloody and unbowed.
If you have just lost the one love of your life, there is no
    possible doubt of it,
They tell you there are as good fish in the sea as ever came out
    of it.
If you are fined ten dollars for running past a light when you
    didn't but the cop says you did,
They say Cheer up think of the thousand times you ran past
    them and didn't get caught so you're really ten thou-
    sand bucks ahead, Hey old kid?
If you lose your job they tell you how lucky you are that
    you've saved up a little wealth
And then when the bank folds with the savings they tell you
    you sure are lucky to still have your health.
Life to them is just one long happy game,
At the conclusion of which the One Great Scorer writes not
    whether you won it or lost it, but how you played it,
    against your name.
Kismet, they say, it's Fate. What is to be, will be. Buck up!
    Take heart!
Kismet indeed! Nobody can make me grateful for Paris Green
    in the soup just by assuring me that it comes that way
    Allah carte.

A NECESSARY DIRGE

≡

Sometimes it's difficult, isn't it, not to grow grim and ran-
    corous
Because man's fate is so counterclockwise and cantankerous.
Look at all the noble projects that die a-borning,
Look how hard it is to get to sleep at night and then how hard
    it is to wake up in the morning!
How easy to be unselfish in the big things that never come up
    and how hard in the little things that come up daily and
    hourly, oh yes,
Such as what heroic pleasure to give up the last seat in a
    lifeboat to a mother and babe, and what an irritation to
    give some housewife your seat on the Lexington Ave-
    nue Express!
How easy for those who do not bulge
To not overindulge!
O universe perverse, why and whence your perverseness?
Why do you not teem with betterness instead of worseness?
Do you get your only enjoyment
Out of humanity's annoyment?
Because a point I would like to discuss
Is, why wouldn't it be just as easy for you to make things easy
    for us?
But no, you will not listen, expostulation is useless,
Home is the fisherman empty-handed, home is the hunter
    caribouless and mooseless.
Humanity must continue to follow the sun around
And accept the eternal run-around.
Well, and if that be the case, why come on humanity!
So long as it is our fate to be irked all our life let us just keep
    our heads up and take our irking with insouciant
    urbanity.

SOURCES

≡

The poems included in this collection were originally published as follows:

Oh To Be Odd! (1931), Money Is Everything (1931), Reflection on
the Fallibility of Nemesis (1931) — in *Free Wheeling* (1931); Spring
Comes to Murray Hill (1930), More about People (1931), Introspec-
tive Reflection (1931), Lines Indited with All the Depravity of
Poverty (1931), A Bas Ben Adhem (1931), Invocation (1931) — in
Hard Lines (1931); The Terrible People (1933), Pride Goeth Before a
Raise *or* Ah, There, Mrs. Cadwallader-Smith! (1933), Apartment to
Sublet — Unfurnished (1933), Look for the Silver Lining (1933) — in
Happy Days (1933); Grasshoppers Are Very Intelligent (1934), Let
George Do It, If You Can Find Him (1935), Portrait of the Artist As a
Prematurely Old Man (1934), Kindly Unhitch That Star, Buddy
(1935), I Yield to My Learned Brother *or* Is There a Candlestick
Maker in the House? (1935), One from One Leaves Two (1935),
Good-by, Old Year, You Oaf *or* Why Don't They Pay the Bonus?
(1933), Are You a Snodgrass? (1934), Roulette Us Be Gay (1935) — in
The Primrose Path (1935); You Have More Freedom in a House
(1935) — in *The Bad Parents' Garden of Verse* (1936); Every Day Is
Monday (1935), Song Before Breakfast (1936), Where There's a Will,
There's Velleity (1936), A Stitch Too Late Is My Fate (1936), Cat
Naps Are Too Good for Cats (1936), To Bargain, Toboggan,
To-Whoo! (1938), Let Me Buy This One (1938), The Song of Songs
(1935), Nature Knows Best (1936), The Anatomy of Happiness
(1938), A Clean Conscience Never Relaxes (1935), The Politician
(1938), A Necessary Dirge (1935), Bankers Are Just Like Anybody
Else, Except Richer (1935) — in *I'm a Stranger Here Myself* (1938); Will
Consider Situation (1940), Procrastination Is All of the Time (1939),
Mr. Artesian's Conscientiousness (1940), First Payment Deferred
(1940), Fragonard (1940), Everybody Tells Me Everything (1940) —
in *The Face Is Familiar* (1940); Dance Unmacabre (1940), A Penny
Saved Is Impossible (1942), I Burn Money (1940) — in *Good Intentions*
(1942); Two Songs for a Boss Named Mr. Longwell (1945), in *Many
Long Years Ago* (1945), appeared originally as Songs for a Boss Named
Mr Linthicum (1931), in *Hard Lines* (1931); We'll All Feel Better by
Wednesday (1949), The Second Month It's Not Itemized (1949),
Nature Abhors a Vacancy (1949), We Would Refer You to Our

Service Department, If We Had One (1948), Thar She Blows (1943), Possessions Are Nine Points of Conversation (1947), I Spy (1949)— in *Versus* (1949); I Can't Stop Unless You Stop *or* Lines Addressed to a Man Making $5,000 a Year Who Overtips a Man Making $10,000 a Year to Make Himself Feel He's Making $20,000 a Year (1952)— in *The Private Dining Room* (1953); MS. Found under a Serviette in a Lovely Home (1956), Ring Out the Old, Ring In the New, but Don't Get Caught In Between (1956), I'll Eat My Split-Level Turkey in the Breezeway (1955), Your Lead, Partner, I Hope We've Read the Same Book (1956)— in *You Can't Get There from Here* (1957); If He Were Alive Today, Mayhap, Mr. Morgan Would Sit on the Midget's Lap (1968), A Man Can Complain, Can't He? (A Lament for Those Who Think Old) (1963)— in *There's Always Another Windmill* (1968); Most Doctors Recommend *or* Yours for Fast Fast Fast Relief (1972)— in *The Old Dog Barks Backwards* (1972).